YOUNG DISCOVERERS

MOUNTAINS AND VOLCANOES

BARBARA TAYLOR

KING*f*ISHER

KINGFISHER
Kingfisher Publications Plc
New Penderel House
283–288 High Holborn
London WC1V 7HZ

First published by Kingfisher
Publications Plc 1992
This edition published 1999
10 9 8 7 6 5 4 3 2 1

A CIP catalogue record for this book is
available from the British Library.

ISBN 0 86272 977 7

Series editor: Sue Nicholson
Series design: Terry Woodley
Cover design: Pinpoint Design Company
Design: Ben White
Picture research: Elaine Willis
Illustrations: Peter Bull Art Studio p.29; Kuo
    Kang Chen p.2; Haywood Art Group pp.4
    (bottom), 15, 24 (left), 25 (right), 26
    (bottom); Kevin Maddison pp.4 (top), 5 (top
    and bottom left), 9 (top right), 11, 12
    (bottom), 14 (bottom), 16-17, 18, 19 (top),
    20, 22 (bottom), 24-25, 27, 28, 30-31;
    Maltings Partnership pp.6-7, 8, 10, 12-13,
    21 (bottom), 22 (top); Janos Marphy, Kathy
    Jakeman Illustration pp.5 (right), 7 (right), 9,
    11 (top left), 14, 15 (right), 16 (centre), 17
    (top right), 19 (bottom), 21 (top), 23, 26
    (top), 27 (bottom), 31 (top)
Photographs: J. Allan Cash Ltd p.27;
    Hutchison Library p.10; Salt Lake
    Convention and Visitors Bureau p.17;
    ZEFA pp.13, 15, 21

Phototypeset by Southern Positives and
Negatives (SPAN), Lingfield, Surrey

Printed in Hong Kong / China
1TR(1BFCJ/0299/WKT/HBM(UNV)/128MA

About This Book

This book tells you all about mountains and volcanoes – what they are and how they are formed. It also suggests lots of experiments and things to look out for.

You should be able to find nearly everything you need to do the experiments around your home. You may need to buy some items, but they are all cheap and easy to find. Sometimes you will need to ask an adult to help you, such as when heating up liquids.

Activity Hints

- Before you begin, read the instructions carefully and collect all the things you need.
- Put on some old clothes or wear an apron.
- When you have finished, clear everything away, especially sharp things like knives and scissors, and wash your hands.
- Start a special notebook. Keep a record of what you do in each project and the things you find out.

Contents

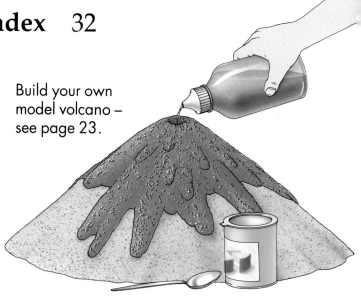

Build your own model volcano – see page 23.

Our Changing World

The ground beneath our feet seems to be fixed and still but really it is always moving and changing. Ever since the Earth was formed about 5000 million years ago, huge forces inside the planet have altered the shape of the land. Mountains have been pushed up. Dust, steam and boiling rocks have exploded from volcanoes. And the lands we live on have drifted around the Earth.

Some changes to the land, like mountain building, happen very, very slowly. Others, such as earthquakes or volcanoes, are violent and sudden. They happen with little warning and can injure or even kill people.

Fire Gods

In the past some people believed that terrible fire dragons or angry gods lived deep inside volcanoes and caused the volcanoes to erupt, or explode.

Where They Are

This map shows you where some of the most famous mountains in the world are found. Volcanoes are mountains, too. They are formed when hot rock from deep inside the Earth leaks out or explodes onto the land. Many volcanoes are in the middle of the sea, but most are along the edges of our seven continents – the Earth's main areas of land.

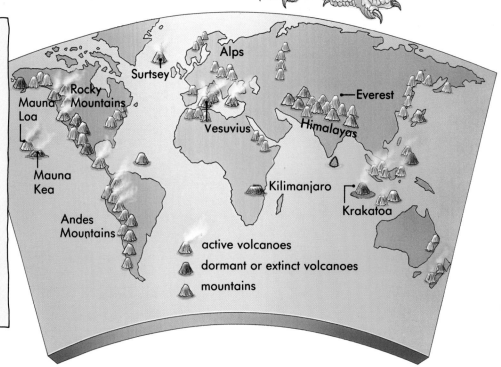

Alps
Surtsey
Rocky Mountains
Mauna Loa
Mauna Kea
Everest
Vesuvius
Himalayas
Kilimanjaro
Krakatoa
Andes Mountains

active volcanoes
dormant or extinct volcanoes
mountains

High in the mountains it can be bitterly cold. Many animals have thick fur to keep them warm. Mountain goats have hooves like pincers to grip the steep mountain slopes.

Studying Volcanoes

The scientists who study volcanoes are called vulcanologists. They try to understand how volcanoes work and predict, or guess accurately, when they will next erupt.

👁 Eye-Spy

Has a can of fizzy drink ever spurted all over you? This happens because the bubbles of gas in the drink suddenly escape when you open the can. A similar thing happens in some volcanoes. Liquid rock under the ground is pushed up by bubbles of gas until it blasts out onto the Earth's surface.

Deep Inside the Earth

The Earth is made up of three main layers – the crust, the mantle and the core. These layers are rather like the skin, the flesh and the stone of a peach. The crust is a thin layer of solid rock. It forms our land and the floors of our oceans. Below the crust the mantle is so hot that the rock has melted to form a thick liquid rock called magma, which is like sticky treacle. The core has an outer layer of hot liquid metal and a solid metal centre.

Scientists believe that the inner core is solid because of the incredible weight of all the other layers pressing against it.

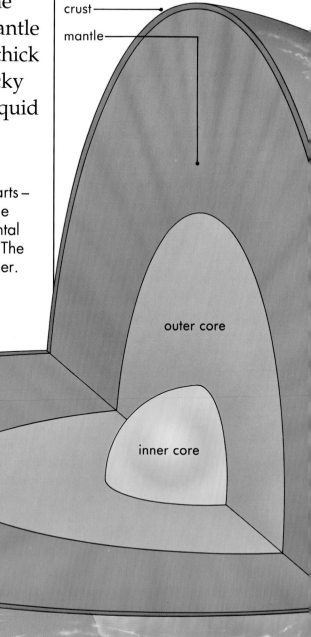

crust

mantle

outer core

inner core

The Earth's crust has two parts – the continental crust and the oceanic crust. The continental crust is about 30 km thick. The oceanic crust is much thinner. It is only 6 to 10 km thick.

continental crust

oceanic crust

mantle

Do it yourself

In this experiment you can make swirling currents of coloured water to see how the magma or liquid rock in the mantle moves around. You will need a small bottle, a large glass jar or bowl and some food colouring or ink.

Inside the mantle, the magma is slowly heated by the Earth's hot core. As it is heated it becomes lighter, or less dense, so it rises up, away from the core. Nearer the Earth's surface it cools and becomes heavier, or more dense, so it sinks.

This happens over and over again, keeping the magma always on the move.

swirling currents in the mantle

1. Fill a small bottle full of hot or boiling water. (Ask an adult to help.) Then add a few drops of food colouring or ink.

2. Carefully lower the bottle into a jar or bowl of cold water. See what happens to the coloured water.

jar of cold water

small bottle of hot water

food colouring

The Earth's Jigsaw Puzzle

The swirling currents in the mantle are so powerful that in some places they have made the Earth's crust crack into gigantic pieces called plates. There are eight large plates and about twelve smaller ones, which fit together like the pieces of a huge jigsaw puzzle. The plates float on the mantle like rafts on the sea, constantly being jostled and pushed by the currents in the magma. This movement of the plates is called continental drift.

Our Restless Earth

Millions of years ago our land formed one big continent. Slowly the land broke apart and drifted around the Earth's surface.

200 million years ago

100 million years ago

Where Plates Meet

Some of the plates are being slowly pulled apart. Others are being pushed together. Sometimes one plate slides below another.

The map shows some of the huge plates that make up the Earth's crust. The red arrows show the direction in which the plates are moving.

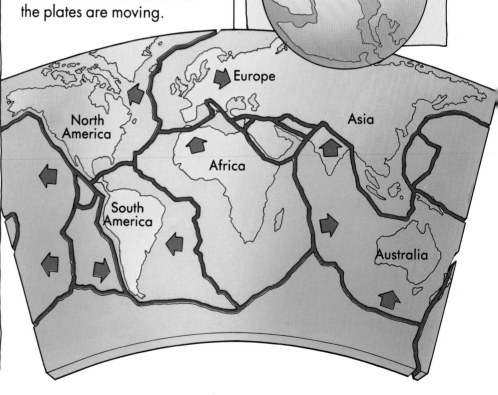

Europe

North America

Asia

Africa

South America

Australia

Do it yourself

This project will show you how the Earth's land once fitted together. You will need a pencil, some tracing paper, scissors and thick card.

1. Find the shapes of Africa and South America in an atlas. Place your tracing paper over the shapes and draw around them.

Clues From the Past

Scientists have found the remains of the same plants and animals on the continents of South America, Africa and Antarctica. This suggests that the land was once joined together.

2. Turn over the tracing paper and trace around the outlines with a soft pencil. Turn it back and draw over the lines on top of the card.

3. Carefully cut out the shapes.

4. Make sure that your cardboard shapes are the right way up. Now move the shapes around until you can see how they best fit together.

9

Earthquake!

As the Earth's plates jostle each other, they put the rocks of the crust under great strain. Sometimes they push so hard that the ground snaps, causing an earthquake.

The point where an earthquake begins is called its focus. Shock waves spread out from the focus like ripples from a stone thrown in a pond. They make the ground shake and tremble and sometimes the land splits apart along a line called a fault.

Buildings like San Francisco's TransAmerica Tower are cone-shaped so that they won't collapse easily during a violent earthquake.

Fault Lines

Once rocks have broken along a fault line they do not join up again easily, so faults are always lines of weakness. Most earthquakes happen in the areas where the Earth's plates join. Take another look at the map on page 8.

One of the Earth's biggest faults is the San Andreas Fault, a tear fault which runs down the west coast of North America. The two other main kinds of faults are normal and reverse faults.

tear fault — rocks slide apart

reverse fault — rocks are crushed together

normal fault — rocks are pulled apart

Do it yourself

How far can you move the blocks of wood (the Earth's plates) apart before the tower falls down?

Built To Last

The Incas of ancient Peru cleverly positioned huge blocks of stone in their buildings so that the walls swayed in an earthquake but didn't fall down.

Measuring Quakes

One way that scientists measure earthquakes is by using the Richter Scale. This scale measures the amount of energy released by an earthquake. A measurement of 4 and above usually causes damage.

The great 1989 San Francisco earthquake measured 7.1 on the Richter Scale. Bridges and buildings collapsed and some people were injured or killed.

11

Building Mountains

The world's greatest mountain ranges are fold mountains. They are formed when two plates push into each other, crumpling up the land between into gigantic folds. Some mountains, called block mountains, are formed on fault lines when great slabs of rock are pushed up between two faults because of movements in the Earth's crust. Block mountains are usually smaller than fold mountains. A third main type of mountain is a dome mountain.

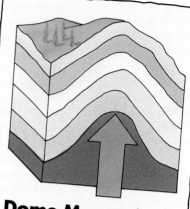

Dome Mountain

A dome mountain is formed when currents in the mantle push up the Earth's crust, making a rounded bulge of rock.

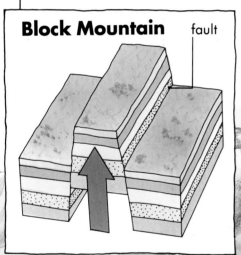

Block Mountain

fault

Sometimes huge blocks of rock may slip down between faults. This makes a valley called a rift valley. The biggest is the Great Rift Valley in Africa.

The shape of a fold in the Earth's crust depends on the strength of the forces pushing the rock and whether the rock is hard or soft. The rocks may be pushed up into an arch called an anticline, or bent downwards into a dip or a syncline. Anticlines make hills and mountains; synclines may make valleys. Sometimes the rock may be pushed right over into an overfold.

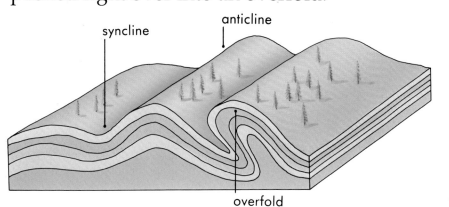

syncline anticline

overfold

 **Eye-Spy**

When you next visit the countryside or coast, look out for folded rock shapes in cliff faces or mountain sides. Road cuttings are also good places to see folded rock.

Young and Old

Older fold mountains, like the Appalachians in North America, are rounded because the surface rock has been worn down by wind and rain (see page 16). Younger fold mountains, like the European Alps, have tall jagged peaks, as shown on the right.

Do it yourself

You can make your own fold mountains. All you need is a long piece of paper, some modelling clay – and your hands!

Put your paper on a tabletop and place your hands at each end of the paper. Now push down and move your hands together. Imagine that your hands are the giant plates moving beneath the Earth's surface. What happens to the middle section of the paper?

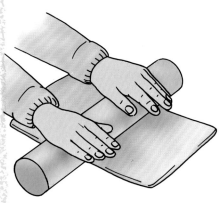

Try making your fold mountains out of modelling clay instead of paper.

1. Roll out three or four pieces of modelling clay. Choose different colours for the layers of rock.

2. Place the pieces of clay on top of each other and press them together.

3. Mould your clay into folds. You will have to push firmly to make your mountains. What happens to the layers of clay?

Famous Folds

All the world's highest mountain ranges are fold mountains. They include the Alps in Europe, the Rocky Mountains and the Appalachians in North America and the Himalayas in Asia.

In 1786, two climbers reached the top of Mont Blanc, the highest mountain in the Alps. This began the sport of mountain climbing!

The Himalayas

The Himalayas are the world's tallest mountains. They were formed about 40 million years ago – long after the dinosaurs died out and millions of years before the first people walked on Earth. The mountains were made when two of the Earth's huge plates collided, pushing up and folding the rock between.

The Himalayas include Mount Everest, the world's tallest mountain. The mountains are still growing, at a rate of about 5 centimetres every 100 years.

'Himalaya' means 'home of the snows'. Only a few hardy insects can survive on the high mountain peaks.

Building the Himalayas

1. Long ago, the plate carrying the land we now call India collided with the plate carrying the rest of Asia.

2. The sand, mud and soil on the ocean floor between the plates was slowly squeezed together and pushed up.

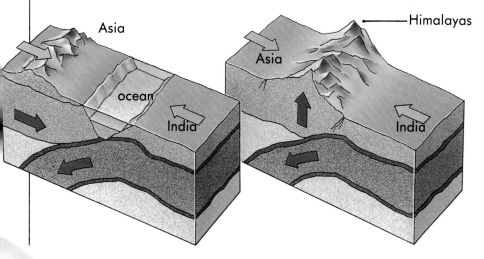

👁 Eye-Spy

If you put some ice cream between two biscuits and try to eat it, the ice cream oozes out. The plates of India and Asia were like the biscuits, as they squeezed the ocean mud and sand.

Wearing Mountains Away

As fast as mountains are pushed up, they are worn down again by the wind and the rain. Rock is broken down by acids in rainwater or by changes in temperature. For example, water seeps through cracks in rock then freezes and swells, breaking the rock apart. Pieces of rock are blown by the wind or washed away by rain and rivers. Broken rock often collects at the foot of mountains, making fan-shaped piles called scree.

scree

Eye-Spy

Fill a plastic container full of water and put it in the freezer overnight. You will be able to see how much water expands, or gets bigger, when it freezes into ice.

water

ice

Plants and Rocks

Plant roots can break up rocks, too. The roots force their way through cracks in search of water. As the plants grow, their roots get bigger and push deeper through the rock, forcing it apart. Some small plants (called lichens) give off acid which eats into rock and eventually turns it into soil.

Do it yourself

See what happens when acid is poured onto rock!

Put a piece of limestone or natural chalk in a jam jar and pour on some vinegar. Vinegar is an acid. It eats away at the rock, making it give off bubbles of gas.

Rainwater contains a very weak acid. Some soft rocks, like limestone, are easily eaten away by acids. The natural cracks in the rocks may become deep channels, forming a 'pavement' of limestone slabs.

vinegar

chalk

jar

limestone pavement

Left: The rocks of Bryce Canyon in Utah, in the United States, have been worn away by wind and water.

Below: Trees roots can hold soil and rock together. When trees are cut down, the soil can be quickly washed away.

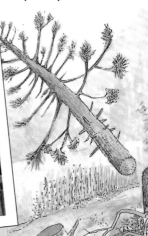

Reading the Rocks

Rivers or the wind eventually deposit, or drop, the sand, mud or stones that they carry away from mountains. This often happens where rivers meet the sea.

The loose grains and pebbles are called sediments and they are built up in layers. Over thousands or even millions of years the weight of new layers piling up on top of the old ones squeezes out any water and the sediments become hard, forming sedimentary rock. You can often see layers of sedimentary rock in cliffs by the coast.

Collecting Fossils

Sedimentary rocks often contain fossils – the hardened remains or shapes of plants and animals. You may be able to find some good fossils on beaches or in quarries where layers of rock have been exposed.

ammonite

Mountain Shells

Fossils of sea creatures have been found in rocks in the Himalayas. They prove that the rocks were once at the bottom of the sea and have been pushed up by forces in the Earth.

A City Fossil Hunt

If you look closely at statues or at some kinds of old building stone with a magnifying glass you may be able to see the fossils of sea creatures in the rock.

Do it yourself

You can make your own fossils with plaster of Paris and modelling clay.

1. Roll out a layer of clay then press a sea shell or a pine cone into the clay so that it makes a clear shape.

2. Mix some plaster of Paris in a clean jar. Carefully pour some of the mixture into the hollow, making sure that it does not spill over the top.

3. Leave the mixture to set hard overnight. Peel off the clay and paint or varnish your 'fossil'!

19

The Exploding Earth

Most of the world's volcanoes are found along the edges of the Earth's plates where the crust is weak. The most violent volcanic eruptions happen when two plates collide and one is pushed down below the other, melting the surrounding rock and making magma. Once magma pours out onto the Earth's surface it is called lava. If a volcano keeps erupting, layers of lava gradually build up around it to form a mountain.

A volcano that often erupts is called an active volcano. If a volcano is quiet for many years, it is called a dormant, or sleeping, volcano. An extinct volcano should never erupt again.

About 50 years ago, lava suddenly began to pour from a crack in a farmer's field, near the village of Paricutín, in Mexico. In just one week the volcano grew about 150 m tall!

Some volcanoes explode with a loud bang, rather like a cork popping off a bottle. When Mount St Helens exploded in the United States in 1980, it tore off the top of the mountain!

How Volcanoes Begin

We still do not fully understand the powerful forces inside the Earth that make volcanoes. Scientists believe that volcanoes begin with magma, or melted rock.

As rock melts, it makes a gas which mixes with the magma. The magma then rises towards the Earth's surface because it is lighter than the solid rock around it.

Eye-Spy

Have you ever made toffee? When the toffee mixture is hot it is soft and runny, rather like the lava that comes out of a volcano. But as the toffee cools it becomes hard. Lava does the same – as it cools it sets into a hard solid rock.

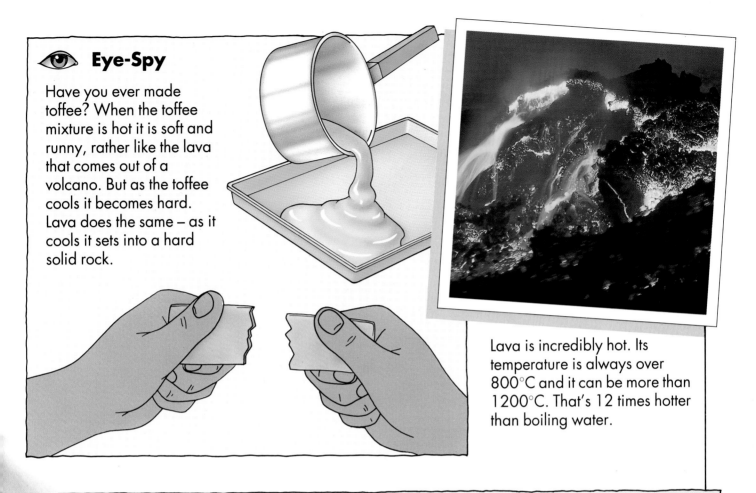

Lava is incredibly hot. Its temperature is always over 800°C and it can be more than 1200°C. That's 12 times hotter than boiling water.

1. Magma rises into the crust where it forms a pocket about 3 km below the Earth's surface. Pressure slowly builds up as the magma pushes against the surrounding rocks.

2. The magma bursts up through weak areas in the surface rock, blowing out tubes called vents.

3. The hot runny lava spills out of the vents onto the Earth's surface. Eventually it cools and hardens into rock.

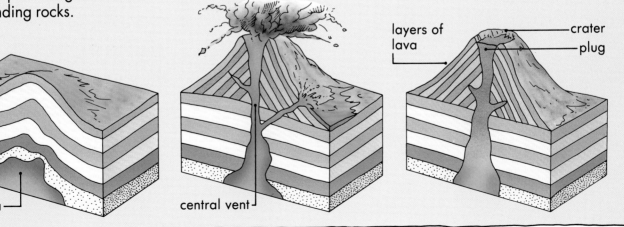

magma

central vent

layers of lava

crater

plug

The Exploding Earth

The shape of a volcano depends on how thick the lava is and how strongly it is forced out of the vent. If there is a lot of gas in the magma, there will be a huge explosion and melted rock, ash and dust will pile up in a cinder cone.

A composite volcano is made from layers of thick lava, lumpy rock and ash. Because the lava is thick, a composite volcano has steep sides. Lava that is thin and runny spreads out to make a low dome-shaped volcano, called a shield volcano.

1. Cinder cone (Mount St Helens, United States)
2. Composite volcano (Mount Fuji, Japan)
3. Shield volcano (Mauna Loa, Hawaii)

In AD 79, a massive explosion blew the top off Mount Vesuvius, in Italy. The city of Pompeii was buried under 6 m of ash and more than 20,000 people were suffocated.

Mount Vesuvius lies inside the caldera, or crater, of an older volcano. Some calderas are made when the top blows off a volcano during a violent explosion.

Do it yourself

Build your own erupting volcano! You will need some bicarbonate of soda or baking powder, washing-up liquid, vinegar, food colouring, a cork or some clay, sand and a tall thin jar.

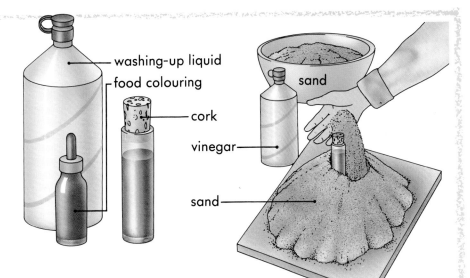

washing-up liquid
food colouring
cork
sand
vinegar
sand

1. Build a mountain shape out of damp sand. It is probably best to do this outdoors or on a wooden board.

2. Put one teaspoonful of bicarbonate of soda in the jar and add a little warm water. Shake the container gently until the powder dissolves into the water.

3. Add a few drops of washing-up liquid and food colouring (red is best) and shake the mixture again.

4. Put a cork or a piece of clay in the top of the jar to stop sand getting in, then push the jar into the sand.

5. Remove the cork and drip a few drops of vinegar into the jar. The acid in the vinegar will react with the mixture to make fizzy bubbles of gas pour out of your volcano like red 'lava'.

soda and food colouring mixture

bicarbonate of soda

Fire Islands

There are more volcanoes under the sea than there are on land because the crust is thinner beneath the oceans, especially at the edges of the plates. Most volcanoes form a huge circle called the Ring of Fire which surrounds the plate under the Pacific Ocean.

In some places parts of the oceanic crust are dragged back down into the mantle and a chain of volcanoes forms, making a range of undersea mountains. Many islands, like Hawaii, are the tops of volcanoes that stretch up from the sea floor.

In 1963, a volcano suddenly burst out of the sea near Iceland, making a new island. It was called Surtsey, after the Icelandic god of fire.

Noisiest Explosion

In 1883 the volcanic island of Krakatoa in Indonesia exploded with such a loud bang that the sound was heard in Australia, 4000 km away. The pink shape on the map shows how far the sound carried.

Krakatoa
Australia

Life on the Lava

The lava and ash from volcanoes eventually breaks down and turns into a rich soil on which plants and trees thrive. Volcanic islands are usually lush and green with plenty of plant life.

Just four years after Surtsey rose from the sea, 23 kinds of birds, 22 kinds of insects and many different plants were living on the island.

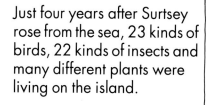

When Krakatoa erupted it caused a huge tidal wave that killed thousands of people.

Ash and lava were thrown 80 km into the sky, blocking out the Sun.

Undersea Volcanoes

Most undersea volcanoes are hidden from view (1) but eventually they may grow tall enough to break through the ocean surface (2). The island of Mauna Kea in Hawaii is actually the top of a mountain higher than Mount Everest!

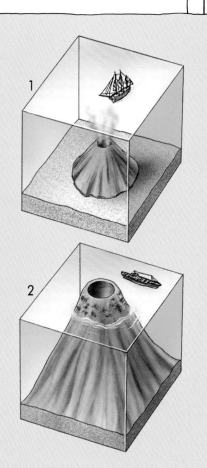

Fiery Rocks

The rocks that are made when magma cools and hardens are called igneous rocks, meaning 'fire' rocks. If lava on the Earth's surface cools quickly, the igneous rocks are hard and glassy with small grains and tiny crystals. When magma cools more slowly under the ground, larger crystals have time to grow.

All rocks are made up of building blocks called minerals and each kind of mineral has differently shaped crystals. Rare and beautiful minerals are called gemstones. Diamonds are gemstones that are found in the igneous rock kimberlite.

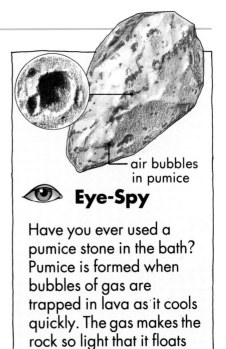

air bubbles in pumice

👁 Eye-Spy

Have you ever used a pumice stone in the bath? Pumice is formed when bubbles of gas are trapped in lava as it cools quickly. The gas makes the rock so light that it floats on water.

Underground Magma

Some igneous rocks form in underground chambers or cracks called sills, dykes, batholiths or laccoliths. We can only see them when the rocks and soil above are worn away.

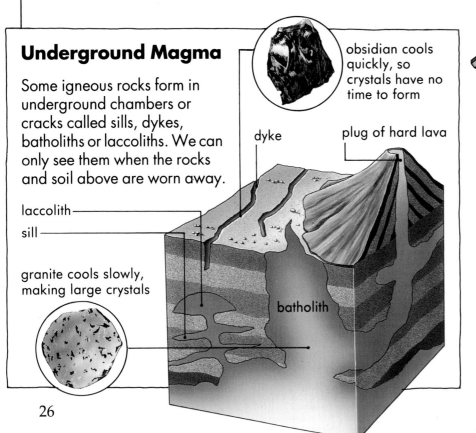

obsidian cools quickly, so crystals have no time to form

dyke

plug of hard lava

laccolith

sill

granite cools slowly, making large crystals

batholith

Do it yourself

Try making your own crystals. You will need sugar, string, a pencil and a glass or jar.

When you stir sugar into a hot drink, it dissolves. Liquid magma also contains dissolved substances. But when magma hardens, the liquids in it evaporate, or turn to gas, and the substances become solid again. This is how crystals form.

Staffa, Scotland

Le Puy, France

The Giant's Causeway and Staffa are both formed from thick lava which cooled slowly into a kind of igneous rock called basalt.

The plug of solid magma left in a volcano is harder than the rest of the mountain. When the mountain is worn away it leaves a tower of rock, like Le Puy in France.

The Giant's Causeway in Antrim, Northern Ireland, is made up of hundreds of tall basalt columns.

1. Heat two cups of sugar and one cup of water in a pan until all the sugar has dissolved. Pour the mixture into a jar and leave it to cool.

diamond in kimberlite

sugar crystals

2. Hang some string into the mixture. In several days, crystals should form on the string.

Hot Water

In volcanic areas where hot rocks lie near to the Earth's surface, pockets of underground water are heated until they boil and shoot hot water and steam high in the air. This spectacular fountain of steam and water is called a geyser. Hot gases also escape more gently through cracks called fumaroles. In the same areas you can often find bubbling hot springs and boiling mud pools.

In Iceland and New Zealand the power from this natural hot water and steam is used to make electricity.

On the Japanese island of Honshu, where the winters are bitterly cold, macaque monkeys often bathe in hot springs to keep warm!

Gushing Geysers

Some geysers erupt at regular intervals. Old Faithful, a geyser in Yellowstone National Park in the United States, shoots a jet of water and steam into the air about once every 70 minutes. It has been doing this for over 80 years!

Yellowstone Park has at least 200 active geysers. Other groups of geysers are found in New Zealand and Iceland.

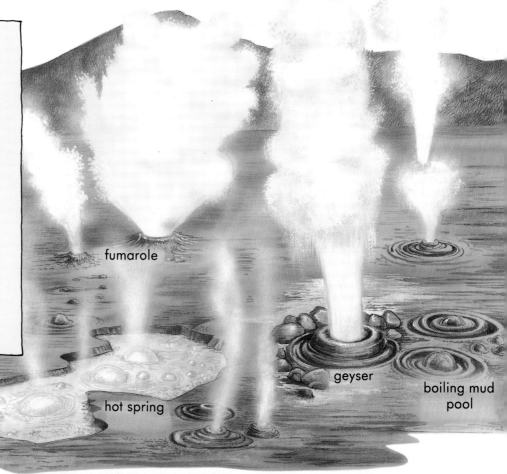

fumarole

hot spring

geyser

boiling mud pool

Do it yourself

Make your own geyser. You will need a bowl, a small bottle with a screw cap, a straw, modelling clay, a pin, and some ink or food colouring.

nail hole through top

Ask an adult to make a hole in the bottle's cap.

cold water

1. Half fill the small bottle with cold water and add a few drops of food colouring or ink.

2. Screw the cap on the bottle and push the straw through the hole in the cap. Seal the hole with clay.

3. Wedge a small piece of modelling clay in the top of the straw and make a tiny hole right through it with the pin.

4. Ask an adult to help you stand the bottle in a bowl of very hot water. As the air inside the small bottle warms up, it will push the coloured water up and out of the straw. How long does your geyser last? To make your geyser work more quickly you could warm the small bottle of water first between your hands.

hot or boiling water

Amazing Mountains

Long ago people believed that mountains were the homes of gods and goddesses. Today we understand more about how mountains are made, but they are still mysterious and special places.

Do it yourself

Why not start a special scrapbook about mountains and volcanoes?

Collect postcards and pictures from magazines, newspapers and holiday brochures (especially for skiing holidays). You may be able to find stamps of mountains from around the world, too. You could also try to find out what kinds of animals and plants live on mountains.

The Yeti

A strange creature called the yeti or the abominable snowman is thought to wander about the distant peaks in the Himalayas. The yeti may look like a large hairy ape but no-one is sure if it really exists.

Climbing Everest

The first people to climb to the top of Mount Everest were Sir Edmund Hillary, from New Zealand, and Tenzing Norgay, from Nepal. They reached the top on 29 May, 1953.

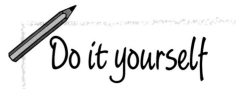

① Everest (8848 m)

④ Aconcagua (6959 m)

⑦ Elbrus (5633 m)

⑨ Mauna Kea (4205 m)

⑩ Mauna Loa (4169 m)

See whether you can discover any strange legends or stories about mountains.

② K2 (8611 m)

③ Kanchenjunga (8598 m)

⑤ McKinley (6194 m)

⑥ Kilimanjaro (5895 m)

⑧ Wilhelm (4509 m)

On Top of the World

Here are ten of the world's highest mountains. The first three are the highest in the world. The fourth is the highest in South America, the fifth in North America and the sixth in Africa. The seventh is the highest in Europe and the eighth in Oceania. Mauna Kea is the highest island peak and Mauna Loa is the world's tallest volcano.

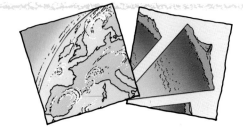

Index